HOW TO TELL
HE'S NOT THE ONE
IN 10 DAYS

HOW TO TELL HE'S NOT THE ONE IN 10 DAYS

Michele Alexander & Jeannie Long

**Andrews McMeel
Publishing**

Kansas City

04 05 06 07 08 BID 10 9 8 7 6 5 4 3 2 1

Library of Congress Control Number: 2003111244

ISBN: 0-7407-4155-1

HOW TO TELL
HE'S NOT THE ONE
IN 10 DAYS

 **DAY 1**

You meet him at a party.

He tells you the girl
he just ditched was his sister.

He acts really interested in everything
you say but forgets it immediately.

He gets you really drunk playing
this new game he made up called "DRINK."

At his place, he offers a massage.

When you tell him you want
to take it slow, he says he does, too.

He talks about the future . . . kids, marriage, target salary.

He says he didn't believe in love at first sight until he met you.

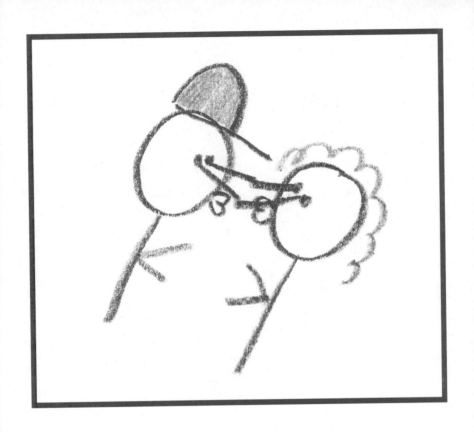

You have sex. (He insists the lights stay on.)

During sex, he complains about wearing a condom.
(They're just too tight.)

After sex, he falls asleep.

 **DAY 2**

He tells his roommates everything. (He exaggerates.)

Then, he tells you he was really drunk
last night and can't remember anything.

He calls you a cab.

He tells you to keep your relationship secret
(because it's so special).

He gives you his card and says call
anytime you want to "kick it cricket."

He says he'll call you later.

DAY 3

He doesn't call.

You constantly check your voice mail.

You call yourself to see if your phone's working.

DAY 4

He doesn't call.

You call your friends and ask if they think he'll call.

You journal about how big of a
mistake it was to sleep with him the first night.

DAY 5

He calls. He says he was thinking about you, but couldn't call because the 7 on his phone was broken. You believe him.

He shows up at your place—late—in his dad's El Camino.

He honks the horn.

He walks five steps ahead of you.

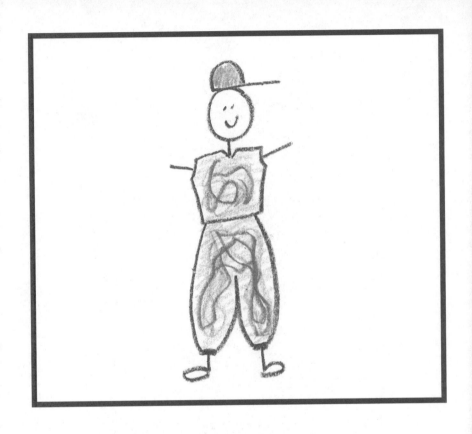

He wears acid wash and pirate-rolls his pants.

He wears more jewelry than you do.

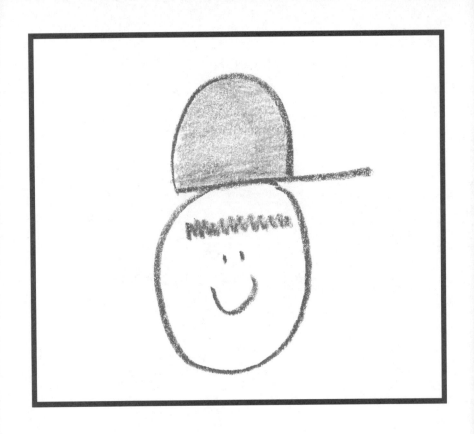

He has a unibrow.

He brags about how rich he is, then makes you
pay for dinner because he "forgot his wallet."

He guesses your weight . . . wrong.

He guesses your age . . . right.

He's an expert on everything.

He takes every opportunity to catch a glimpse of himself
(e.g. a mirror, a store window, a pond, the hood of his car).

Anywhere you go, he talks about
how cool it would be to have sex there.

He constantly checks out other girls.

After dinner, he has nothing else planned and you
sit in the car for an hour debating about what to do next.

He insists you play "I never" and pushes you for details.

Before sex, he tells you the reason he hasn't committed is because he hasn't found the right girl yet. (He insinuates you're it.)

He tells you that kissing is boring and a waste of time.

During sex, he gets you to try out new positions.

When sex is over too soon, he says it's
because he can't control himself . . . you're that hot!

And it's a relief to not have to
worry about petty conversation.

DAY 6

When you get up to go to work,
he won't wake up no matter how hard you try.

He tells you he doesn't have a job . . . he's in a band.

He invites the rest of his band over for a jam session.

They get drunk and pass out on the couch.

When you get home, he asks, "What's for dinner?"

He says that he and his friends are going to a party and you're welcome to tag along (and bring some hot friends).

He makes you drive.

At the party, he starts every sentence
with "dude" and ends it with "bro."

He ignores you (unless he needs a drink).

He introduces you as his designated driver.

He refers to himself as "the man."

He has his friends come up
and refer to him as "da bomb."

He starts a fight with the weakest guy there.

He constantly one-ups you.

He only laughs at his own jokes.

He tells you that the girl across the room who's
staring at him is his ex and she stalked him and
he hopes you're not a psycho like that.

Before sex, he constantly asks
you how many guys you've slept with.

During sex, he says he can't kiss you because
he doesn't want to get sick (even though you're not sick)
but is more than willing to do everything else.

He never "returns the favor."

After sex, he sneaks out and goes back to the party.

DAY 7

He shows up, unannounced . . . drunk . . . with a pizza.

He makes you break all plans for a romantic day together.

You watch *SportsCenter* and he shushes you.

He borrows your shorts and
brags about how baggy they are.

He gives you pointers on how to better yourself.
He suggests you join a gym.

He farts and says it's because
he feels so comfortable with you.

He plays pocket pool.

He refers to high school as the greatest time of his life.

He insists you call him by his nickname, Trigger.

He shaves his head and says
it's time for a tougher image.

Before sex, he asks you to take a shower.

After sex, he takes a shower.

DAY 8

He borrows money from you.

You give him a job lead.
He says, "No chick's gonna change me—love it or leave it."

You decide to leave it. He sits outside your apartment
in his car for six hours and stares at your front door.

When you leave, he follows you with his lights out.

He goes to a party and gets really drunk.

He booty-calls you.

He tells you he misses you and
quotes cheesy lines from movies.

He says he's ready to change for you.

He regifts a bottle of wine that has
a card attached to it that says "Love, Monica."

During sex, he asks if he can tape the
experience so he can remember it forever.

 **DAY 9**

He takes you to a postcoital breakfast.
He uses a coupon.

He flirts with the waitress, then doesn't tip her.

He accuses you of flirting with everybody.

He suggests a three-way to liven up your sex life.

You notice his back-ne.

He drives with his elbow out the window
and plays air guitar on the steering wheel.

He wears mandals.

He refers to you as his old lady.

He doesn't include you in any conversation.
If you try to speak, he raises his voice higher.

You realize his boobs are bigger than yours.

After sex, he tells you he wants to marry a virgin.

DAY 10

When you start making plans for the weekend, he's vague.

He tells you things are moving too fast.

And he says this whole "relationship" thing was your
idea and he has no clue what you're freaking out about.

He explains the difference between
"dating" and "hanging out."

He still tries to have sex.

When you say "no,"
he says he never liked you anyway.

That night, at a party, he glares at you while
making out with another girl. And he tells all his
friends that you're still in love with him.

You drink a beer and start back at DAY 1.